Poetically

Baring my Soul

Poetically

Baring my Soul

Jerald Brown

Whilst every effort has been made to ensure that the information contained within this book is correct at the time of going to press, the author and publisher can take no responsibility for the errors or omissions contained within.

Typesetting by *www.wordzworth.com*

This book is dedicated to Tierra L. Brown.

What I owe you far outweighs these pages.
I appreciate your unconditional love for me.
I am honored to have been blessed with a
child as wonderful as you. Your maturity
motivates me.

Acknowledgements

Thank you, God, my strength, my peace, my love. To You I owe everything. You blessed me with this gift. I honor You with my writings.

Thank you, J.W. and Dizer Brown, for your love, your support of whatever I chose to do, your guidance, and your wisdom. I love you both!

Thank you Tierra L. Brown, my lovely daughter, for inspiring me. I love you dearly!

Thank you, Tiffany, for your words of encouragement, your integrity, your devotion to the Lord. I look forward to our next conversation!

Thank you Gabrielle, for enduring the years of my real life soap opera! You've witnessed more than most. No words can accurately express my gratitude. Let's put a face to the history!

Thank you to everyone who motivated me in some form or fashion to write this book.

Contents

Preface

First of all, I want to thank God for the privilege to write this book. This opportunity took over 5 years to embrace, but thankfully I accepted this challenge to express the poetic gift God has given me. Fear never prompted my hesitation, for I (we) don't receive the spirit of fear. But rather, I hadn't recognized my potential before, nor had I ever considered writing a book.

I can cite several sources of inspiration for this documentation. Undoubtedly, God precedes the list. He not only blessed me with this gift, but He initiated the call to write, publish, and distribute this book. My daughter, Tierra, is another that inspires me. She has a gift of poetry herself, and the energy, passion, and innocence she carries within excites me every time I read her poems. I have a spiritual mentor who encourages me to present my talent to the world. I have a very good friend in Virginia that keeps me on the realm of reality when I sometimes attempt to move about the twilight zone. My surroundings, family, upbringing, and community motivate my writings on a level that I'm able to capture on paper.

Poetically Baring My Soul is probably no different than any other poetry book, except for the fact that the author is relatively new in this field. What I bring to the public is literally my spirit, soul, and body, all being expressed poetically from my heart. This book is not meant to indicate whether I'm prolific or not. This is not an attempt to win any sort of prize or be highly publicized. *Poetically Baring My Soul* is an offering of my gift, to be shared with poetry lovers everywhere.

This book is divided into 3 sections: spiritual writings, soul poems, and in bodily format. I am a child of God. I understand that I am a spirit, I have a soul, and I live in a body. Therefore I felt, what better way to communicate poetry to the people than through the areas that make-up man? The spiritual poems are more of recognizing God, implementing scripture to the poetry, and just glorifying the Lord, honoring Him and loving Him. The poems of the soul deal more with relationships, past and present. Since the soul is made up of your mind, your will, and your emotions, the reader can expect from this section all of the above being touched. The body section pertains more to the community, metaphoric usage, wordplay, a little humor, and descriptions of life in general.

Use *Poetically Baring My Soul* for whatever the mood calls for. Maybe you want to praise God for certain blessings but you might not know how or what to say. Maybe you've never experienced love to the magnitude being felt, and you wonder if anyone else has achieved that level of love. Maybe you like poetry with confidence that sometimes borders on arrogance. This book will definitely apply to one of these areas and more.

I appreciate your time, support, and acceptance of this literary work. I pray that I am able to stimulate you with at least one of my poems. I thank God for the blessing, the guidance, the direction, the strength to complete this book. The poetry came easy. The book development was the challenge. But I stood, and stand, on what the Word says: "I can do all things through Christ Jesus which strengthens me." (Phil 4:19) Thank you, and enjoy your reading!

A SPIRITUAL

CONNECTION

You Deserve My Praise

You deserve my praise
For letting me breathe
With You with me, there's nothing I can't achieve

You deserve my praise
For helping me to witness the truth
It's acknowledged as I solicit the youth

You deserve my praise
For being my light in the dark
Clearing my vision so I wouldn't stumble nights in the fog

You deserve my praise
Cause even when pains would hurt severe
You told me how to persevere, Lord

You deserve my praise
When my spirit was cold and lifeless like death in December
You accepted this sinner

You deserve my praise
Cause my mama's a blessing to the world
Truly my heaven in the form of a girl

You deserve my praise
For my father being consistent
His discipline and his wisdom kept me out of imprisonment

You deserve my praise
For giving me a daughter
Who has taken after her father
With ambitions of being a scholar

You deserve my praise
For allowing me to be Christ-like
Born in the flesh, now I'm about to be given life twice

You deserve my praise
For your continuous lifts
I'm so unworthy of your numerous gifts

You deserve my praise
For my truest friends given
I will prove this while I'm living
I'll be true until my ascension

You deserve my praise

For Your blessings from above me
I do not doubt You, but how did You manage to love me, Lord?

You deserve my praise
For making me the man I became
And sending Your Son to keep me out of the flames

You deserve my praise

Looking at Life

The Holy Spirit's guiding me.
God's light is shining on me.
The world's way is no longer blinding me.
Looking at life, now my eyes can see.
The sun is brighter.
The grass is greener.
The world is lighter.
The sky is bluer.
The water is clearer.
The air is cleaner.
The birds sing melodically.
Work comes easier.
Old friends leave faster.
Family judges more.
The world's persecution increases.
Love is stronger.
Peace is abundant.
Smiles come more often.
God is realer.

How I Love Loving You

I've fallen in love with You. Since the moment I sought after You, our continuous fellowship elevated into intimacy. My thoughts stimulate my emotions as I think of all of the wonderful ways You've expressed Your love to me. Sometimes I feel unworthy of such adoration. There's nothing I won't do for You.

My willingness should indicate how I love loving You. My heart smiles as I please You. I enjoy our daily encounters when we interact. Are You as excited as I about spending quality time? When we converse, Your Word continuously edifies my spirit. I surrender myself completely. I plan on loving You forever!

I sacrifice my life for Your sake. The world has noticed how you've changed me. I don't care! All I care about is You. I delight myself in You. I represent You. I'm lost without You. In Your absence, life has no meaning. Let me serve You. I insist! Heavenly Father, how I love loving You!

I Was on His Mind

When God created the Earth, I was on His mind
When mankind was given birth, I was on His mind
When grace was made abundant, I was on His mind
When the world became my circumference, I was on His mind
When He sent His Son as the sacrifice, I was on His mind
When He wanted to show that nothing else could match His life, I
    was on His mind
When the Holy Spirit descended like a dove, I was on His mind
When the chapter in His Word taught us about love, I was on His mind
When leadership and teaching were bestowed as gifts, I was on His mind
When the wisdom of His Word was sent to uplift, I was on His mind
When He knew I felt alone, He sent my own "Eve." I was on His mind
When God's love gave me air because in sin I couldn't breathe, I was
    on His mind

But When You Walk With God

Sometimes we take for granted the brilliance of the sun or the calm of still waters as though they have no significance to our lives. Often times we are deafened by the unmelodic sounds of life's calamities and we uncontrollably dance to the beat of that drum.

But when you walk with God….

The sun does more than provide light. It radiates the area's circumference and warms the cardiac of the cold-hearted. The quietness of a stream indicates nourishment for the sheep. As wool-haired creatures thirsting for wisdom, the peace of the brook invites all those in need of a drink. If strife troubles the water, they'll evacuate the pasture.

When you walk with God….

Any troubles that fall upon you won't entangle you, for you comprehend that the Lord is the puppet master, not the circumstances. So your dance is equivalent to a ballerina's. The music is somewhat of a spiritual seduction in that, as we embrace the harmony of God as our leading conductor, His direction entices us to intertwine with the notes of reassurance and give faith an affectionate kiss.

The True Meaning of a Soldier

A soldier protects. A soldier risks his or her life for the cause of righteousness. A soldier is obedient to the orders given by the commander in chief. God is the commander in chief! He prepares us for war; spiritual warfare. His tactics are perfect! His strategies are impeccable! He provides the keys to victory. Let us dress for war!

God's soldiers wear armor unlike any other; we are fully dressed for protection. The belt of truth securely wraps around our waists, which upholds our character. The breastplate of righteousness protects our hearts from all of the enemy's tricks. Our feet are fitted in custom designed boots to help us move swiftly in the gospel of peace. Our shield of faith extinguishes the flaming arrows shot by evil. Our minds are guarded with a helmet of salvation and our indestructible weapon is the sword of the Spirit, which is the word of God.

We pray in the spirit, we're alert at all times, and we persevere through all battles. We are soldiers! This is our life! This is what we do!

This Is Who I Am

This modern day Roman
Is witnessing modern day wickedness roaming
Even amongst so called believers
Subconsciously believing that, because they observe the law, they're safe.
But it isn't observation but justification by faith.
We have to be transformed by the renewing of our minds
And understand that it's God's design
For us to be more than conquerors
The world wants me to support their ways, but I can't sponsor them
Honestly, that old man wants to rise up
And question why they're staring, trying to size me up
I'm hoping they start attacking!
But that can't happen
What I want to do, I do not do
And if I do what I don't want to do
Then it's no longer I who's doing it so I can't do that!
Say that three times!
And I can care less how you critique this Corinthian
Because it's still love, because God is
In Him is my protection, in Him I'll persevere
In Him is my trust and in Him is my hope
I'll reflect patience in your pressure and kindness in your provoke
The old me has passed away, I am a new creation
I'm an heir according to the promise so I am Galatian!

Long as I'm breathing, this Ephesian
Will put on the whole armor
And serve Him whole-hearted
You may think I'm tripping but this Phillipian
Knows that by petitioning and prayer
And thanksgiving in the air
My requests can be presented
Reassured that I can do all things through Christ which strengthens
First, Timothy said if I provide for my family then a hero stands
Second, Timothy said God didn't give me the spirit of fear so I fear no man
And it isn't like my high priest hasn't experienced what I've been through
Matter of fact, I could never withstand what He went through
So my faith remains
And it's pleasing to God and His faith sustains
As I walk in obedience I'll be missing the flames
Receiving blessings through perseverance because I listened to James
I'm still a man, I still feel pain, and I'm still a soldier
But, God told me to cast my anxieties on His shoulders
And here's one thing you'll never have to question
My walk is a representation of God's reflection
So go ahead, judge me, and bring your slanderers

I was preordained in this walk before there were calendars
Some of y'all lacking faith too scared to stand in the lion's den!
Your bosses come like goliath; you're intimidated by "giant men"
But hold up, I know I got issues
And it's not just wishful thinking that I hope to be blissful
But let me confess
If I was Adam, I probably would've taken a taste
If I was Abraham, I wouldn't be the father of faith
To sacrifice my child? I'm left in bewilderment
With my Israelite attitude, we'd still be walking in the wilderness
I don't sing abundant songs of praise, but my mama does
I am not anywhere near as wise as Solomon, but I thought I was
But I'm growing under grace daily
To leave His Word you couldn't pay me
The enemy's game couldn't persuade me
You can persecute me and call me crazy
Born again, look at the new baby!
Respect what it is, this is how He made me

This Is Who I Am

Don't Let These Tears Fool You!

You witness continuous streams flowing from the face of a man that within your mind you've regarded as the picture of strength. Confusion, surprise, and a fraction of disappointment begin to cloud your judgment of me as you replay the countless times I've offered up reassurance and encouragement in your own personal situations. Your amazement and wonder of my watery pupils elevate thoughts of what could've crippled my stand up demeanor. Your extension of your shoulder to lean, your requests of any type of support I'm in need of, your own display of sadness because of the Charmin I've been utilizing, shows your commitment to assist in the resurrection of the happiness that you've experienced from me time and time again.

But don't let these tears fool you!

What you're envisioning is the unexplainable joy I've found from being reborn into a kingdom that is always providing me with love, honor, and peace! All of the wonderful blessings that have been bestowed upon me when my thoughts process His goodness are showing themselves in an outward projection that cinema just can't duplicate! I drop the tears of a child that has realized that sin's cataracts have been removed! I am no longer attached to the world's respirator, no longer breathing in the air of violence, fornication and drunkenness! Thank you for your concern, but there's no need. Each tear that you see is just my inner self being cleansed! God has forgiven me my transgressions, He remembers my sins no more, and He has chosen me to be an intricate part of His family! I am so grateful!

As Long as I'm Breathing

As I inhale the wisdom of God with every flow of the Word's air, my inner being expanding to the capacity in which it was created to function from that moment of breathing in,

Watch as I exhale the fruits of the Spirit that has been circulating within since the birth of this true son, allowing that immediate mist to provide a fragrance in which those who encounter it delight in its fruity sensation.

As I inhale the positive comments and confidence that are displayed in the atmosphere because of the trust and admiration you bestow upon my persona,

Watch as I exhale the leadership that you undoubtedly witnessed throughout our short life span together.

As I inhale your teachings of responsibility and ownership without choking on misconceptions and pride,

Watch as I exhale the reflection of maturity and brightness because of the light you deliberately shined on me.

As I inhale the oxygen of love that you exemplify every time we interact with each other, be it spiritually, business wise, or conversation,

Watch as I exhale the same air of love with actions that collaborate with your thoughts, plans and desires.

I Never Tasted Fruit like This

How thoughtful of you to feed me! I have to admit, this has never been done to me before. I used to see it happen in the movies, but that's not even equivalent to this display of affection. I really enjoy the variety of food you brought into my life. I never tasted fruit like this. Allow me to describe each taste:

Love; like a mandarin orange. Once you get a taste, you never want to let it out of your life.

Joy; like it's straight off of the cherry tree. I love how its juices flow through me.

Peace; green apple flavor. I can't describe the calm that's being digested within.

Longsuffering; like sweet, seedless grapes. From this fruit, patience is definitely a virtue.

Gentleness; ooohhh! Chiquita bananas! I really love this taste!

Goodness; pineapple mixed with peaches. Now this is what I call a taste of Heaven!

Faith; like thick, ripe strawberries. It's so sweet to be faithful.

Meekness; tastes like plums. There's uniqueness about being kind.

Temperance; now, that's like watermelon. You can never go wrong with some self-control in your life.

Reflections

You are me……I am you.

You worship God……I praise the Father.

You adore Jesus……I love Christ.

You spend time with the Lord……I meditate in His Word.

You are passionate about the Word……I yearn for His wisdom.

Your fruit is ripened in all seasons……My fruit is delivered fresh daily.

You look to the Lord for guidance……I acknowledge God in all things.

You have God's glory dwelling within you……I've been baptized with the Holy Spirit.

Your intimacy with God enlightens me……My appetite for knowing the Father touches you.

Your right……Is my left.

Your joy……Is my excitement.

You long to enter the gates of Heaven……I intensely plan to stay out of hell.

Your t.v. only knows spiritual channels……my t.v. is purposely locked onto bible teaching ministries.

You have thoughts of concern for me……I have thoughts of your welfare.

You exemplify God……I walk in His Word.

You look at life through God's eyes……I see reality more clearly since God is with me.

You love me……I love you.

Your Choice Became My Blessing

All things stem from a decision. We are encountered with choices every day of our lives. Your intentions were to perform a job, not to impact a life. Your effort to assist in the growth of a company became paralleled with guiding a lost soul to salvation. You never asked to make an acquaintance with any associate. Actually, initially you didn't truly wish to make that connection. Troubled by a desire to offer help to the individual, you acknowledged the Lord. Lo and behold, His answer began the transformation from darkness to light. Yes, your choice became my blessing.

I definitely never expected to meet a true child of God. Countless others claimed to be, quoting scripture after scripture, but their actions didn't quite match their words. My blindfold became evident after several conversations with you. Before, I believed to have found the true path. Thank you for removing the knot of the scarf from over my eyes. Thank you for helping me to adjust to the light. You didn't have to help me. You could've easily denied the challenge. Maybe there is_ something about me! With your obedience to Him, there couldn't be any other decision to be made. Now, the sun seems brighter, the grass greener, the world lighter. Your choice became my blessing.

Inseparable

In the same respect to a mother and child, there's no separation of you to the Father.

As symbolic as the critical connection of Siamese twins, if severed, one would have to lose their life. With Jesus living forever, your existence would be the fatality.

I am a witness to the spiritual umbilical cord displayed as your growth is manifested from the food of the Word.

You acknowledge Him in all things. He is highly esteemed above all other loved ones. Although He needs no defense, you attempt to protect His name against the slanderers.

Whenever you walk, His comfort is seen around you. Joy radiates as you introduce Him to those who don't know Him. He's always no more than a prayer away.

Lying in bed, you embrace His warmth. In early mornings, secluded from everything else, you await His instruction. You follow His lead. You obey His decrees.

You love Him for who He is, and He loves you for who you are. He declared He'll never leave you. You show that you always belong to Him.

Like a branch to a vine, air to the lungs, and the head to the body…...

Inseparable.

Maybe She's Out There

I'm looking for my spiritual mate. Maybe she's out there. The woman out to capture God's own Heart; like the law in search of a fugitive. And she has no understanding of what "useless" is, because she's determined. Reflecting God's beauty, she's confirming His Word as His Truth acrobatically leaps from her tongue when she speaks! Her spirit, overflowing with an abundance of joy because our circumference employs an identical commitment to upliftment of God's Kingdom. Her smile, would display His Radiance. She'd have me around here singing cadences like nursery rhymes! But this isn't about no Jill and Jack running up a hill and back! This is about our aligning ourselves to God's Will! In fact, I LOVE the way she loves scripture! Her assurance of eternal life because she knows it's hers! Her attraction to the fact that I'm making absolutely for certain that I'm going by a revealing, and not a feeling. Because you know our emotions change like the weather! We could be partly cloudy one day and a tsunami the next! And I'm not trying to go through what a tsunami suggests so spiritually, we need to be in the same forecast. A sunny, 77 degrees with a slight breeze so I can serenade her under the right trees with the Song of Solomon. She'll be intrigued at the way I harmonize with him, so … .

I'm looking for my soul mate. Maybe she's out there. The woman who'll allow me to become her comfort. Giving her that security when the weight of the world comes unannounced. Letting my love blanket her as she curls on the couch and my warmth is elevating her temperature. But she's ok. She's just remembers the July's trifling men treated her like Decembers and the fever she's experiencing is her sweating out their infections. Her stares give an example of our whole

connection. And her arms… strength similar to Samson's… squeezing gently around my waistline, means that she takes time. No, as a matter of fact, she makes time to show me that she's my foundation. On any given day you'll see me tongue kissing the clouds or dancing on the horizon. Hearing me clearly without the use of Verizon that I love her unconditional! Nowadays it's untraditional for a madam to become Adam's Eve because Adam wants Tina, Latoya, and Angela or maybe even a Steve! And Eve desires the affection of a Christine! But I'm not with that! I want one woman to cleave so we can eventually become one flesh. At least that's the goal in mind. Because I would want our souls to climb and she would want our souls defined so we'd know each others' roles to play. And mine is to be her provider, be her help meet, her best friend, her ministry; her shoulder to lean when depression's consumed. And my shoulder's broad enough, she'd have plenty of room! And what our minds would consist of, and our wills have chosen, with the correlation of our emotions is that God's Way is our focus. Then what WE want will be given to us as well. Look….

I'm looking for my life mate. Maybe she's out there. The woman who'll embrace my dreams and not consider a 9 to 5 a finality. And yet, clear up any confusion I may have with reality. The woman who'll kiss me with truth when pride attempts to seduce me because usually, that's how we are as men. WE think the sword is mightier than pen! WE think her intuition don't weigh up to our logic until we get like R Kelly and get trapped in the closet and can't sing our way out of that garbage we fell in! No! I want the woman who'll intertwine her faults with mine. Who'll accept my imperfections. Who don't mind taking heed to

*my directions because she knows they line right up with God's! When,
our longing for one another would outweigh the arguments. And we'd
face any challenge together, no matter the consequence. I need her to
understand that divorce is not on the guest list! It has no place in the
building or for what I'm building! So I need her to stimulate me. Speak
His Word to regenerate me. Bring increase to my life productively. Sing
to my spirit so seductively that she touches me without touching me!
Where are you at love? I can't see you. I don't know... maybe she's out
there.*

SOULFUL
EXPRESSIONS

I Can't Help But Stare

You are so beautiful to me,
Your inside is as radiant as your outer frame.
I can't help but stare,
The captivation along with the longing for you is now the same.
Attracted to your sexy magnetism,
I can't seem to escape your pull on me.
If you embrace what I believe you've been wanting,
In time I guarantee that you'll know me.
As I stare into your photograph,
My world starts to enter a twilight zone.
My equilibrium is shaken up, my focus is off,
But my thoughts are "why would I want to fight this zone?"
My prayers have been answered,
Your smile appears to truly be directed at me.
There's something about this particular picture,
The rapid beat of my heart shows I'm affected, you see?
Can you hear my thoughts? What are they screaming?
Are you in agreement with what's on my mind?
When I look deeper at your presence attached to film,
Your demeanor would indicate that you're giving me a sign.

Yes I'm attracted to you,
I've been that way from our genesis.
And it's not just from a picture,
I pray that you've been sensing this.
But your devotion to the Lord is what I love most,
I'm so fixated I won't boast,

But I can't help but stare.

The Things You Do To Me

Touch me.
Hold me.
Kiss me with your conversation.
Please me.
Capture me.
Attract me with no complication.
Assure me.
Console me.
Seduce me with that smile in your picture.
Complete me.
Intrigue me.
Connect me to you as we bond through scripture.
Move me.
Subdue me.
Impress me with your intellect and wisdom.
Astonish me.
Enlighten me.
Make me dance to your lifestyle's rhythm.
Befriend me.
Ascend me.
Give me thoughts that God sent you for me.
Bless me.
Revive me.
Caress me spiritually giving God all of the glory.

Touching Without Touching

It's not amazing nor surprising that I'm able to feel you at any point of a 24 hour period, no matter the distance. Your actions have inadvertently applied pressure to my heart. The concerns you have towards my well-being indicates that I, too, indirectly touch you as well. I'm impressed! As we continue to walk towards God, we welcome the spiritual embrace provided by each other's friendship and allow it to heighten our senses, impact our emotions, and cause our spirits to rejoice even from merely saying hello. My thoughts are often grasped by your lifestyle and certain decisions are made based on your patterns. Of course God is acknowledged first! I don't have to shake your hand to know that you respect me. My tears don't have to be wiped to understand your care for me. Hugs aren't necessary, for we comprehend the affection that binds us. And kisses? Not applicable here. That passion is felt every time we discuss the Word. The further the discussion, the more passionate the kiss.

I Don't Want You to Leave

I stare at you and my heart smiles
Your eyes whisper for me to take my time when incorporating quality
I listen to your laugh and I hug the sounds
Your laughter is appreciative of my insistence for more
I love when we rendezvous in my thoughts throughout the day
Keep letting your fragrance kiss me softly
You touch me with the closeness we're beginning to achieve
Although we just got here, I don't want you to leave

I labor without fatigue when building our relationship
I've been looking for your particular type of merlot for some time now
As we drink in the wine of each other's company
We become intoxicated by each other's realness
I always expect to complete you
I'm learning as I feed you, I've been satisfying your appetite
You're the reason everyone notices I smile more often
Although we just got here, I don't want you to leave

Hours move like minutes, which compromises our fellowship
I make the most of your head on my chest
You rejoice as I taste your entire personality
I embrace how you return the favor
Feel how my mattress accepts your presence
What we share is intimate, yet poetic

To answer your question, yes, I'm all yours
Although we just got here, I don't want you to leave

You're a fixture in my future, you abide in my heartbeat
I pray that you never relocate
What you've done is arrested my soul
I can't picture a better portrait than us
I develop a new level of patience during your absence
And I fantasize of the next time you bring warmth to my evening
I speak from my heart and purposely massage your emotions
Although we just got here, I don't want you to leave

How long will you stay with me?
Can't you tell that my music is lonely without your lyrics?
If I had an explanation, I would say I'm being selfish
But I enjoy how your fullness discourages my emptiness
I'm motivated by your perfume that still lingers on my comforter
And I reminisce of all the connections we've made
What's funny is, we just met yesterday
And although we just got here, I don't want you to leave

Come Dance with Me

Come dance with me. Take my hand and let us partake of the rhythm. As you stare in astonishment, I sense an attraction beginning from the smile you display. Although others have been cast away, there's something about me that edifies your confidence to trust in this request.

Come dance with me. Allow me to take the lead as we connect with the emotions caused by the music of our hearts. You move like you've longed for someone to match your steps. I've impressed you completely with my ability to keep up. So seductive in our movements, outsiders are captivated. It was known from the genesis that the two would become one flesh.

Come dance with me. Let the music intoxicate you. Witness the emptiness of the room. Focus on my stare. Cherish this as our song. Tighten your hold on me. I won't let you go. This is our night. This is our life. Come dance with me.

Let Us…..

Let us plant our seed of friendship. As the sun enlightens us and the air of each other's company continues to circulate, stimulating life to come, we will blossom into what God has preordained us to be. Although we cannot predict our future's outlook, I believe the beauty of our common rose will fully develop because of the cultivation of God's Word, leaving each other amazed at what has been created as we stare at each other's petals and smile at one another's accomplishments.

Let us paint our picture of life. Together we become so artistic because we share an understanding of the colors of our dreams that we are determined to achieve. Each stroke we apply to the canvas of the world shows how perfectly we interact with one another. We can't help but to develop a masterpiece! We don't care about what the critics think. The way we choose to paint our picture is the way we choose it. Personally, I don't believe that anyone else's opinion matter, nor can they frame our portrait!

Let us build our house. Of course the foundation has to be the Word! Otherwise when the winds of hate and the rains of despise beat against it, it won't last. Next are the walls of true friendship.

The strength of the framework should be cemented with laughter, support, respect, and trust. As we attach the roof, remember it has to be high enough to where we won't bump heads with our beliefs, and be solid enough to provide continued protection from the vultures that will prey on our growth, because they lack that kind of bond. Now we can add all of the things we need for living comfortably in this house: peace, love, commitment, sacrifice, and desire to see each other prosper before our own personal selves. Then it will be a home!

October 3rd

This is the day that the Lord has made.
This is the resurrection of my life.
This is the birth of my future.
I began to experience love.
I started my readjustment on living.
I received one of God's blessings.
My reflection was manifested into the earth.
My transition was made from boy to man.
My priorities were redirected.
We celebrate this gift that was bestowed upon us.
We honor this day with adoration.
We rejoice in its truth.
The next level emerged.
The beat of my heart extended.
The love of my life appeared.
My daughter was born.

Her Character Touched My Soul

Beautiful! The description from that one word barely taps into the essence of this blessing that has conveniently bonded into my home. There's no cross reference I could use to illustrate the depth of emotions I feel because of our recent connection. I mean, as recent as 2 weeks or 14 days or 336 hours or 20,160 seconds!

She has inadvertently touched my soul with her dynamic character. My impatience is obvious because of numerous messages I send in her direction. I'm anxious to receive her responses, or just to see my name behind the word, "hello." I hear her melodic voice repeatedly harmonizing over Whitney's and I realize that "I have nothing!" My heart rate is in constant fluctuation whenever I think of her, envision her smile, or substitute my loneliness with her emails.

In my reconciliation with God, He has seen fit to increase me with a woman whom I can utilize to maintain peace throughout my day, and who unknowingly brings delight to my evening. I focus on her ability, her desire, and her determination to be the woman God created her to be and that in turn motivates me to be better than I am. I stare at her portrait and she blushes. I witness her lifestyle and appreciate God that much more. Her strength is a testimony to the trials she's had to face, and I applaud her with my tears. Little does she know, she's made a friend for life. Her character touched my soul.

In Memory Of

I can remember a connection that was first established by a mere glance towards the direction that heaven was standing. Nervousness became the immediate emotions flowing through me. But as intoxicating as I am, I knew it wouldn't be hard to break the ice and pour her a glass of my Hennessey conversation. I must admit, she was very capable of handling game's liquor. So I added a few shots of tequila flirts and jokes to loosen her up. By the end of the night, we ate from each other's wordplay and concluded with a warm embrace. Drunken from keeping in good company, we blacked out, unaware that what had transpired was the beginning of love.

I can recall anxiously awaiting those late night phone calls. The pain from the wait continued growing closer by the day as if I were truly experiencing labor. The contractions were more than I could tolerate so in that respect, I salute all women of the world! Your voice was all that was needed to encourage my personal storms to drift away from me. You are strength, without bulging muscles exposed to the earth. Your posterior is so well sculpted that even under the biggest robes, your persona is enough to move mountains by simply reading a book or smiling at a gesture. Your letters were elegantly written. Our weekends displayed weekends of passion and inevitably introduced you to love's true meaning.

Unfortunately, we're now at a loss. Those feelings are now deadened and I am totally responsible for your demise. Forgive me, for my transgressions were not of a sane man's conscious. Your essence was murdered, though not intentionally, in every degree of existence. This

I have to carry with me until I breathe no more. As you started to feel alive, I weakened you with disease of selfishness. The more you wanted to grow and blossom, I, your sun, continued to hide in the clouds, neglecting you of light and warmth. Hopefully in the next life, you can reflect off of the past and establish 360 degrees of true love, peace, and happiness. Farewell.

Now I Realize You're Not Coming Home

June 1, 2002. It's been approximately 8 years since the disappearance of love and on this day, I've come to the realization that you're not coming home. As I stare through the window of time, I want to open it and pass through in order to return to a past that illustrated our love, and reposition the pieces so that feeling could remain the same today. Unfortunately, all I can do is stare at old memories.

Actually, love was diagnosed with a disease called street life years earlier and the symptoms had begun to expose themselves rapidly. Over exposure to gang fights, underdeveloped sense of manhood, aches and pains from a companion putting his "friends" first. Several experienced people in this field explained that devotion to family is the only cure for this disease, but the ignorance eventually assured death of a relationship due to deterioration of support.

Too late for the tears; what's done is done. There's no bringing back what death has claimed. Inside, I scream to God for one more chance to do right if He gives love back to me. But The Creator allowed for love to dwell in a new place. The happiness is evident after the final kiss. No more old pains. No more weakening moments in the middle of the day from lack of support. Only the new life ahead, with no looking back. I'm missing you. But now I realize that you're not coming home.

Or So It Seems

Attractive with a magnet's pull
Beauty as magnificent as the strength of the light of the sun
Amazingly causing a momentum shift of the beat of my heart
Your voice unknowingly disrupts my balance
I'm overwhelmed by your southern smile
Seduced by the kiss of your giggles that touch my ears from laughter
    of my unwitting humor
You have captured me in a cocoon of peace

Don't be blown away
This is more of a gentle breeze
Dancing this kite in your direction
Expressions being exhibited through the colors life allowed you to envision
Emotions causing your elevation into completeness because you embrace
    the whispers of this moment
Thoughts of "I've never floated like this" continue to change your focus
Now you're not hesitant to touch the sky
You can feel the clouds hug your inner being
I've dazzled you for a day
You've been tampered with for life

From What Mine Eyes Have Seen

You exemplify God from your walk to your speech
You exhibit His wisdom to everyone within reach
You are a blessing to those that's considered a brethren
You wear a smile that's symbolic to the description of Heaven
You are a beauty that's unmatched by the natural woman
And your spirit is beyond the catch of the natural woman

You are truly a child of God
And you move me without a pause
As I mimic your warm shine, I notice my future's bright now
I pattern myself after the tapestry of your lifestyle

I'm convinced that your home life testifies to your obedience
You illuminate God's glory from the way you handle grievances
I'm honored to make your acquaintance, I rejoice in the continuity
For having dialogue with an angel is a rare opportunity
As a moth, I enjoy basking in your light
You should be the blueprint of the passion you have of Christ
And I notice you're the spiritual pillar to your colleagues
I find myself defending you from misguided souls who make mockeries
Cause they're clouded by the spirit of strife
But from what mine eyes have seen, knowing you could only bring
    them to life

Heaven in the Form of a Girl

Breathtaking! Never would I have visualized paradise until I made your acquaintance. Your illumination reached out to me and I couldn't help but to embrace it and walk towards you. I certainly wouldn't have thought it was time for me to leave this dismal world as I knew it and enter into your kingdom. But my approach to you felt so good! So I left the "earth" to be completely consumed by your love.

I've dwelled within your bliss for approximately a month now and I must say that beautiful is a vague attribute compared to what you display. I keep in remembrance that it is forbidden to become intoxicated so I attempt to sip daily of the wine's elegance you promised that flows through your river of love.

I can see why so many are trying to get to you. I, myself, am very attracted to you so I could only imagine how others who once obtained entrance into your kingdom feel, now that they've been banished from you forever. I don't feel sorry for them because you've gave them countless chances to receive you and they decided themselves to remain sinful.

I hope that my good endeavors outweigh the bad. You have the utmost decision whether or not I'm able to remain within or be exiled. But either way, I have the honor of experiencing Heaven in the form of a girl.

I Can't Have Her

I can't have her. Timing's not right. Her frame's picture perfect.
   Her smile's contagious.

I'm longing for her. Her stares scream connect to me.
   Uncontrollable lust occurs. She's also attracted.

I speak her desires. She seeks intimacy. Others don't weigh up.
   She envisions our future.

I can't break the rules. She reaches for my soul. I breathe in her virtue.
   Her maturity scares me.

Thoughts of her flood my day. I stimulate her growth.
   She belongs elsewhere. We're beginning to elevate.

The path narrows for us. We continue to accelerate.
   Our bond's becoming cemented. We don't know what we're doing.

Further attention's requested. We see better at night.
   Affiliation's achieved. I just kissed her spirit.

I can't have her. Timing's not right.
I can't have her. She belongs elsewhere.
I can't have her. I can't break the rules.
I can't have her. We don't know what we're doing.
I can't have her.

Not So "Inappropriate"

Caressing her soul; Cradling her heart; Tasting her wisdom;
  Not so "inappropriate"

Captivating her life; Kissing her spirit; Embracing her rhythm;
  Not so "inappropriate"

Accelerating her breathing; Arousing her emotions;
  Capturing her significance; Not so "inappropriate"

Inhaling her beauty; Increasing her thoughts;
  Celebrating her magnificence; Not so "inappropriate"

Wiping her tears; Strengthening her faith; Accepting her brethren;
  Not so "inappropriate"

Completing her smile; Being her testimony; Giving her Heaven;
  Not so "inappropriate"

Deleting her sadness; influencing her movements;
  Seducing her totally; not so "inappropriate"

Pushing her skyward; Cultivating her gradually;
  Pleasing her, hopefully; Not so "inappropriate"

She Smiled, I Fell

I can't believe this has happened. My attraction to this woman has left me in a state of emotional clumsiness. From my initial contact, my swagger began staggering as if sobriety was an issue. But for Jay? Me? I couldn't blame it on the alcohol. You've got to understand. See my bishop status is hereditary and my pimping magic is legendary! I could bless them and undress them in a February sun! Every stroke of my genius brings convenience from the mattress to the subliminal! But what I encountered was almost criminal because what she stole from me was my ability to stand in her presence. I took one look into her glory and when she smiled, I fell.

Totally unexpected! Completely unsuspected! As many opportunities I've rejected to become a significant other, I couldn't understand how I had come to embrace this! But in retrospect, I wouldn't replace this. You see, her smile was just the genesis. She had the walk of a runway model, with a corporate conversation that sometimes bordered in seductive consultation but she was humble with it. Her spiritual is so biblical; I can recite her life story in the form of any scripture you can think of and it exactly matches her description. Her actual physical portrait is so beautiful; I could close my eyes and connect the dots to her silhouette. Lay her across my comforter and keep my pillows wet with her insight. And even as my pen writes poems, I realize this woman is poetry in itself! Even though I grabbed her attention with my rendition of what she does to me, every time I noticed her smile, I fell.

So now I'm beginning to drift, contemplating thoughts to submit to her will. I listen intently as her inside voice announces her appreciation of my air and the more I'm around, the deeper she breathes. The more I astound, the deeper she needs me to keep being real. Keep giving her that extra. Keep reminding her that I'm more than just a poet; I am hers and all that that implies. I keep looking up at the skies with my back against the earth with no desire to reposition myself. No desire to recondition the wealth I have in her because you see, I'm comfortable laying here. For the rest of my life I'll be staying here, if she lets me. Hopefully she'll be joining me on the ground we respect as mutual and in our future we'll look back and laugh at this past moment. Celebrating about this past moment when we smiled at each other and we both fell....in love.

Seduction

Do you like this papaya taste? I won't stop feeding you. I need you to continue enjoying the juices that intend on flowing forever. I can't help but attempt to extract any juice left from your lips in hopes of embarking in a passion that would allow us to become wrapped in a cocoon of overwhelming emotion. I won't stop feeding you. I believe you'll never get full.

Let me massage your soul with the anointing that has been gifted to me. I am truth, manifested in your presence to provide you with a touch you've never experienced in all of your years of breathing. As my realism presses against you, you begin to witness muscles being relaxed, after countess others brought on a stress caused by fakeness, hurt, and immaturity. I see that you're starting to love this touch! The sounds of pleasure are being expressed as I move throughout your much needed temple. I'm opening up your thoughts. You appreciate my movements. I won't stop until you tell me to.

Can I kiss you? I don't mean just any kiss. This is one of paradise being introduced to you in the flesh. As you allow my tongue to caress you by the words I whisper, lips articulating my every letter, I want you to envision lying on clouds. I want you to embrace every tingle traveling inward. Allow me to apply an inspiration of love that your inner self can appreciate. Cheer as this type of tongue kiss gently resurrects what you believed to have been deceased.

You scream out your love for me in your mind, not wanting to confess this verbally…..not yet! I want to kiss your spirit to the point of combining ours together. I'll always occupy your space. I believe you'll kiss me back.

Lie in this field of roses and let our eyes dance to the beat of our hearts. Your smile indicates you accept this invite. Your touch shows you want more than stares. The racing of your heart says you love the fact I belong to God. You sense no fear with me. You thank God He sent me to you. The gentle breeze entails our peace with each other. You've never felt like this before, huh? Only one word describes it…..seduction.

Needing You

I am so far off of the Earth, its ridiculous!
Your love is so infectious, I'm so sick with this,
Yet I insist in this because
I would rather succumb to the death of the old me
Than to continue to allow my soul to be
Rotting as I walk or dying as I breathe.
You are the answer to my prayers, the wisdom as I read
The arms to my sleeves, the oxygen to my survival
You are the song Solomon sung in the bible!
Listen as I duet with him
Our sounds are so parallel; it's obvious I'm equivalent with him
And you are content with him
Or rather, Jerald

Because he has become your world
And you reinforced his
Because you are is rib
In his attempts of giving you a second one
He has affected some of your life as he honors the Perfected Son
And you neglect him none of the time
Actually, your reflection comes with the shine
He increasingly illuminates because of you
He literally wants to become one with you
Comfortable

Sharing the exact same atmosphere
Declaring the exact same stratosphere
As our mattress
Flying to no particular address
Riding with no vehicular access
No gas tax, no traffic, just us
Celebrating the justice of just us!
Do you know how long I've been seeking you?
How strong my desire is of completing you?

I want you to complete me too!
Give me weak knees too!
You don't understand. You have me like Angela Bassett
From a man's perspective
For so long I've been waiting to exhale so now I'm seeing
That as my chest swells, I'm truly breathing!
Impatiently waiting on my Nextel to bless well with your voice on the
*   other end*
I'm walking around like I've graduated and others' have expelled!
With you in my life, I've only excelled!
Your love has me under a sex spell!
I'm still thinking of sex tales from 2 weeks ago!
I'm not trifling, I know I should've changed the sheets, you know

But while I'm snuggling, don't get it twisted, I'm reminiscing
And what my pillow cases are whispering is real pillow talk
You've left footprints on my emotions and I still feel the walk!
I know you think is game or it's smooth as your latte
But what I'm giving is that unconditional, that agape
That God type of love that I continually practice
That makes you want to do continuous back flips
Because I gymnastically excite you; you recognize our yoke as equal
If you view this love as a motion picture, just wait until I promote the
    sequel!
Don't let hatred eclipse where this light shines
Don't ever disconnect this lifeline
Don't ever neglect the eternal tick of this life time
Just promise me you'll comfort my zone, love
Promise me you'll comfort my home, love
I seek you
I plead you
I believe you
I breathe you
I need you

So Much in a Sunrise

The awakening of the spirit; you are the glow of life being manifested. You shine light upon every living creature within your circumference. Your morning stretch exceeds the stares that are cast in your atmosphere and you begin to brighten the lives of your personal favorites... including me.

The warmth of love; you express yourself with just the right temperature to produce an energy unexplained. As we embrace your splendor, we rejoice in your presence because you have given in abundance heat that comforts when you speak to us. Every touch is relevant to our life force. You truly enhance life.

A focus on life; I, for one, could never take for granted the powers you have to not only add to, but multiply my existence since you've shown your glory to me. Never have I experienced this type of reality. I grow because of you. Breathing is so natural because star, you've made it so. And just imagine, this only begins my day! I appreciate you. Don't stop showing your true self to me. I bet you didn't know that there's.....so much in a sunrise.

I EMBODY
GREATNESS

The Purpose of My Being

First and foremost, I am a living examination; a test from birth to death to establish a place within a realm that is regarded as the highest point of elevation.

I am to acquire knowledge from all walks of life, in order to establish wisdom enough to give a total understanding to whomever wishes to learn from me.

I am to lead within a jungle where wildlife has overcome a vast majority of these streets. I feel that this "navigator" has enough drive to carry any passenger through this rugged terrain, as well as against the elements of nature.

I am to be responsible for any and all of my actions and deeds, along with the upbringing of my children. The seed is only as good as of the plant that which it came.

It's a must that I spread game in all of its forms to those under my tutelage. Ignorance of these laws will not be a way of life for those under my influence and teaching.

I am determined to use my life to resist the powers that be in their attempts to use their strength against my people for their own selfish needs.

I am to stand firm on the foundation of my beliefs and principles, and also support those not capable of standing up against the wrongdoings of mankind.

I am to live according to the rules set by the Creator, thereby denouncing all negativity within my circumference. Satan tries to tempt me at times, but my repentance is evidence that his path will not be followed.

My purpose is to give love, respect, and honor to the black women of society. Without "u" there would never be an "us." Paying tribute and homage is a continuing part of my life, and I will strive to fortify you in such a way that your reflection will blind those who belittle you.

I am here to provide after I'm gone a presence that will be stained on the hearts and souls of many that I was as real as they come.

So, Tell Me Something?

So, tell me something? Is it the baritone my voice displays that gives off an attraction unexplained between two people whose play on words finds intrigue amongst us? My belief is we were connected in our past lives; perhaps my bear to your honey, my bee to your dandelion, my sun to your earth. Whatever, however, whenever, we have a belonging.

So, tell me something? Can you picture life with a man with a professor's intellect, a thug's swagger, a soldier's heart, and the Spirit of God within? I will prophecy my completion of you. Look me in my eyes and accept this love. Embrace us as we elevate to a realm unbeknownst to man.

So, tell me something? Should you not trust the extra beats of your heart or the chills of your skin when you breathe in the air of my company? Do you know what that is? That's love giving birth to love. It was premature, but it has grown into a prosperous being, reliant only on God and the activities between us.

A Description of Truth

Elegant; Trustworthy; Beautiful; Determined;

Passionate; Honorable; Firm; Dynamic;

Intelligent; Eternal; Funny; Confident;

Supportive; Focused; Straight-forward; Strong;

Poetic; Skillful; Significant; Important;

Unlimited; Expressive; Grounded; Believed;

Undeniable; Natural; Fortunate; Priceless;

Healthy; Established; Real; Felt;

Consistent; Non-fictitious; Friendly; Necessary;

Enlightening; Wisdom; Understanding; God

The Great Debate: His Truth or My Truth?

So, me and my guys were playing dominoes the other night, politicking about life and reflecting on our pasts; how we all stood on the common ground of the ghetto streets we frequented and as delinquents we practiced shooting everything from dice to 4-5's; from jump shots to game! Staying in the lane of being street V.I.P's where our reputations were our signatures! We were proud of those stigmas! Proud of being understudy's to the literature of block lessons! Amidst confessions of slightly missing yesterday, the conversation of our congregation turned in a different direction. Where they were boldly glorifying the boulevard, I was glorifying God for His Hands of protection for those days. I was thanking God for His rescue while they were celebrating about death dues our fallen comrades had to pay.

As I called out for 15, I don't know whether it was hatred or ignorance that formed a cloud of seriousness within the room as the attitude of one of my guys starts flaring. He said, "Who're you supposed to be, a pastor now?" and he was laughing loud as he attempted to belittle me. He said, "You act like you ain't affiliated! Trying to come off like you're rehabilitated from banging! Homie, violence runs through your veins! It's purified through your arteries; properly, I might add! And where was your so-called relationship with God when your hustle was on? You know Mary Jane was your hustler's song! The revenue from that residue kept your safe overflowing!" But I'm slick ignoring him as I continue the game and I keep my man on lockdown, all the while I'm scoring like Jordan in all 6 of his victories and they're sick of me getting it in! As I holler out "10!" frustration is elevating because the man who started this

54

conversation isn't concentrating on holding me down. I looked at him and asked, "Are you finished yet?" But he was getting replenished when he sees I get a text from a friend of mine I need of some extended time. He said, "And your love of God ain't more than your love of women! I've seen you leave clubs in any subdivision with either a number from a wife, to a lover for the night! You can miss me with what you're trying to twist me with! You might be able to tangle them up, but I know better! Homie, you ain't being real!"

The silence that followed seemed to suffocate the moment. But I'm focused! My opponent is obviously intoxicated from that third glass of Hennessy, but that's his last taste! Plus, I look at the score and this fool is in last place! So after I made my play, I made my statement and I came as real as the air we breathe. I said, "First of all, I'm striving for faithfulness, not perfection! My connection is based on acceptance of His Son, the will to walk after Him, the choice to repent from my walk within sin, and not to be discouraged when I face my trials. As far as gang life is concerned, not only am I rehabilitated, I'm liberated because I'm affiliated with Christ! Timothy reminded me that in my violence, I was shown mercy because of my ignorance and unbelief." He said, "Timothy who?" I said, "Never mind, because you're spiritually blind!

And yeah, I used to run the streets getting my grind on, getting my shine on! I still have a hustler's ambition, but my hustle's transitioned! My mission is to reciprocate real estate, not flip weight! You don't see me go to the block no more because I don't want to be CEO of the block no more! I want to incorporate corporations! I want to be the vessel God

blesses to be a blessing to others. And so what if I'm attracted to women? That in itself isn't sinning, but the difference is, back then I was only looking for nights of sexing! Now I'm seeking life with my best friend! A wife as a blessing! And you're tripping over my life? Wow! You've been divorce twice now! So, what does that say about you?"

Now he has the hush mouth! And I just robbed him for 20 points, needing 10 to roll. It looks like I just hurt his soul! But while he was trying to knock me, pitifully, I knocked him literally! And I'm knocking him, and I'm knocking him, and the man across was like, "Ain't no stopping him!" and before I was about to win, I looked at my debater and said, "Now, whenever you want another lesson in my faith or these ivories, you confide in me and we'll entertain this little rivalry! But for now, y'all got to go!" Domino!

Confessions

Confession #1: I didn't like you during our first encounter. In my mind, you were the enemy. Me and my supervisors never seen eye to eye. I judged you before I knew you. But look how good God is, though! You became my best friend. You showed me how to listen to instruction. Your patience humbled me.

Confession #2: I never expected to be as close to you as I am. Your position not only states that you refrain from personal relationships with associates, but I carried an inner despise for management and past dialogues were based on frustrations, complaints, and a lack of care towards the company. You know more about my life than most of my closest friends and family members. You've seen me operate in every emotion, from laughter, to sadness and crying, to anger, never ashamed of expressing myself to you.

Confession #3: I never had a friend like you. Anyone, whom I called a best friend, never introduced me to Jesus. All those who claimed they loved me, never persuaded me to establish a relationship with God. Everybody that claimed to have my best interest at heart left me alone when I decided to follow God. But it's o.k., God sent me you. I cherish the time we spend discussing the Word. I'm grateful for the time you took to help me when I needed it. You're the best friend I ever had!

Lost Innocence

Shorty's got to hold his own

At 13, cause his poppa was a rolling stone.

And since that became the plan of the spouse,

The child's hustling; he got to play the man of the house.

And he don't really know much about God yet,

But he understands his struggle in the projects.

And the young man's strapped, walking around dressed in steel;

It's a must after witnessing his best friend killed!

Mama's fiending for a heroin fix!

Teachers' constantly telling him he'll never be….shhh!

Crooked cops want to see him deceased

Because his reputation's growing, they don't want him being king of the streets.

The penitentiary is calling his name. Who are the fault and the blame?

With no guidance he's eventually caught up in the game.

There is nobody trying to teach him

So I'm saying this poem from my heart, hoping that I reach him

She's thinking that life actually isn't fair.

Lacking a father figure because her daddy wasn't there

Baby, you're being blinded by no guidance being given from your pops

You're determined to be hitting the block.

You just discovered what your S.E.X. is!

Thinking you are grown until you're thrown in the back of his Lexus!

The sex is overwhelming your precious womb, thinking you love Jones,
You let this man hit with no glove on
Cause 26's he's sitting on them
Candy coated paint and that paper he's sitting on some bank.
You're fascinated by the way he works the corners?
Wait! His next intention is to make you work the corners!
Hey! Didn't you know that you were God's daughter?
You don't have to sin to eat!
You don't even have to be in them streets, investigate your purpose!
Breathe, baby, don't be suffocated by these men's abuses,
Cause they don't need no excuses
When they're smacking you up!

I Hold Myself Accountable

My daughter grew up without her father. Not because I wouldn't be bothered, but because what I honored was street life. Violence became my delight and darkness would ultimately be light, in my mind. Communication was nil throughout her years. My immaturity was more than ill, it was sickened and my will was stricken with irresponsibility. I didn't connect with her abilities, her gifts, and her passions. I can clearly see rejections when I'm asking, "How's school?" "What are your future plans?" "Who is this so-called future man you've been dating?" She feels that I hate when I attempt to teach game and she feels I'm too late and she don't want to hear it. It seems she don't love me like she used to, but I hold myself accountable.

I wasn't the man I thought I was but heaven seen that my fornication at 17 brought forth a blessing I never dreamed of gaining back then. I should've followed my father's example of sacrifice for us, but no, I was running around in fights and wars in the streets trying to gain fame. But my daddy didn't gang-bang, he maintained! And I'm ashamed because, she shouldn't have to struggle for nothing, she's my only seed! Suffocating under excuses, if I would only breathe! Focus solely on what she only needs! If she resents me, I don't blame her. If she's hurt, it's because I've pained her. If she doesn't grow, it's because I didn't raise her, didn't cultivate her, didn't motivate her. Thank God for His grace and mercy! I get an opportunity to replace what hurts me! And that's what hurts her. I didn't mean to desert her. But as a child I thought like one, I walked like one. Now enlightened with bright wisdom, I walk like the sun! Or better yet, I walk like the Son, Jesus! Please, it's forgiveness I seek from You and Tierra!

Please deliver me from this stormy weather! From the tension these odds may seem insurmountable but since I hold myself accountable, I know that's step one to recommitment. Forgiveness brings clarity to resentments. Our conversations defeat the pain's growth. This is my covenant and her smile completes the rainbow.

My Way with Words

Here I come!
Watch for conception in 7 days!
Next Saturday night it's official!
Referees can't charge me with a 3 second violation!
Attempts at incarceration are pointless!
Hollow points cause damage to the chest cavity!
There aren't procedures for fillings or root canals!
Let the water flow towards its destination!
I'm headed for Heaven!
Paradise on earth is the ultimate goal.
Touchdown! I've achieved victory!
Or I'm dead in my accomplishments as I've lived.
Breathing an air of righteousness; sometimes choking on pride.
It goes before destruction and comes before the fall.
The autumn leaves fall on my daughter's birthday gift,
It's life!
Given twice, I'm living eternally this time!
No Rolex needed to watch!
I see the prize in front of me, it's glorious!
The beauty can't be captured on film!
There's no $5.00 matinee to witness!

Speak Jehovah's truth to the spirit!
Become edified! Keep building up!
Upkeep the building in case company comes!
I incorporate a style you can't fashion into sense!
Add 2 more to the 5 that's common—book and street!
These avenues I rep till it's over, with Griggs on my shoulders,
I military press your hatred, no matter the weight!
I'm too obese for your slander!
Your ridicule is ridiculous, but it's not comedic!
Richard Pryor is turning in his grave!
Please let him rest in peace!
It transcends all understanding.
Do you comprehend my wordplay? My skill is absolute!
It's not mixed with cranberry juice, it's straight 80 proof!
The evidence is clear, he's guilty!
My conviction to being real is unmatched!
You better change into the right colors!
My Crayola years paint pictures of my innocence.
No involvement in snitching for cheese!
God made me human, not rat! Call Terminex!
If somebody doesn't control these pests, my home will be vacant!
I empty out my savings to follow my dreams.

Let me awaken my spirit when God whispers.
Soft spoken but His words are abundant in nature.
Dandelions, eagles, and trees give praise.
Forever and ever, let the church say amen!

You Might Want To Get Some Practice

Somebody told me you are a legend. That you're elite with the game you have. Well you know what they say, actions speak louder than words. Let's see!

I hope you can handle the bounce because if not, expect to be stripped! Someone of your caliber, I don't foresee you crossing over. You appear to be a straight to the lane type of player. Well, I'm dynamic when it comes to defense and my vertical won't allow you to pump fake.

Don't mistake it; I don't underestimate your skills. But I rebound off of every brick you throw up and "Iverson" answer from beyond the ark! I AM SPALDING!

Oh, and you're free to throw your shots at the line, cause your "Shaquille" attempts allows me to "Wilt Chamberlain" our game. Matter of fact, I repeatedly receive 3 second violations from laughing so hard!

I love your competitiveness! You're really striving for a championship ring, huh? Well, being the Taurus that I am, it's only natural that I have 6. You seem awestruck from the human highlight dunks I'm giving. I'm the inspiration behind the Jordan logo! See me fly! Should I cut the nets down now?

That's Not What You See

Sneakiness? In my eyes? That's not what you see. The fact is you've come across someone who isn't intimidated by your seduction. You've intoxicated many with your champagne vibes and you anticipated another alcoholic. But I bubble just like you! In fact, my Dom Perignon style exceeds your J. Roget level! Maybe you ought to upgrade.

Me? A player? That's not what you see. What you're looking at is confidence manifested within a humble demeanor. Your expectations of me being hypnotized by your video vixen are deluded because I'm the B.I.G. Bad Boy! I went from ashy to classy, yet your attitude's still as nasty as your girl who gladly wanted to call me daddy by the end of the night. I love it when they call me big poppa! But don't worry; my faith is melodically suggesting that if you act right, you may get one more chance, baby, baby!

The Other Side of the Pillow

Honoring God

The air in the Garden of Eden

A gentle breeze

A light summer rain

Autumn's evening

My demeanor

The other side of the pillow

(cool)

Who Would've Thought?

Straight A student; Comic book collector; Music lover; Piano player;
Who would've thought?

Gang-banger; Alcohol abuser; Disrespectful; Father at 18;
Who would've thought?

Army veteran; College dropout; Dope seller; Gang chief;
Who would've thought?

Penitentiary destined. Deadbeat father; Part-time worker; Woman
seducer; Who would've thought?

Christ connected; Accepted sinner; Child of the Father; highly
favored; Who would've thought?

Experiencing God; Born leader; Humbled spirit; Full-time employee;
Who would've thought?

Poetic soul; accomplished author; Father-daughter relationship;
One-woman man; Who would've thought?

What Is There To Talk About?

No, don't try to come home now! Mama always said the grass may be greener on the other side, but it still has to get cut! Now you see the snake for what it is! You left me for a Morris Chestnut fantasy, only to connect with a Franklin! Or Wesley! Talk about a disappearing act!

You let infatuation come in between our love. I sacrificed my time to help you buy a house! Faithfulness should be tatted on my chest in regards to us! I committed myself to being the father figure your kids couldn't fathom from their own deadbeat dad! How could you? Why did you?

Now you want to talk, huh? Why? You found out his wife knows where you live? Can't stop her from cutting them tires? She stays ringing your phone off of the hook, huh? What? You been thinking about me? For what? You left me months ago! How do you miss me? I was the best thing that ever… .you know you got some nerve… ..! You know what? Don't even trip. Stay where you're at and enjoy the yard! Ain't nothing else to talk about!

Pound for Pound

I am more than a contender!

I'm a human highlight with continuous play on Sportscenter!

You're not ready for my endurance!

My reputation suggests stipulations of back-up as insurance!

It's victory or death! These streets got me sparred up!

It's firearms in these gloves, either way it's arms up when it's over!

People judging on your corner like Harold Lederman

Now you're standing on your corner hemorrhaging

Truly bleeding the block!

And I'm old school, 15 rounds partner!

Ruffling featherweights, you can't fit these pounds, partner!

Match me!

You're a technical lay-down, cover up!

Gamblers bet it all on me and double up!

Partner, you're the one who decided to press conference the fans

And couldn't deliver any of them threats promised the fans!

You should've tightened your mouthpiece!

Now my combination's got you literally outreached!

Ringside and out weeks!

What Are You Searching For?

I woke up this morning exhausted! Not from manual labor from the day before. This fatigue actually started from way before from weariness of being broke for years. Lying in my bed, nearly close to tears, my frustration had been building and I'm tired. I'm tired of needing extensions before my lights get cut off! And I'm tired of needing financial relief before my life gets shut off! And I'm tired of having a job but I'm still borrowing money! And I'm tired of feeling undependable! And I'm tired of not enjoying life but I'm pretending to! And I'm tired of hearing the voice of a disappointed daughter! And I'm tired of my immediate family still being supported by my mother and father, in other words, I'm fed up! So, as I'm laying there in my despair, I hear a voice and I'm clear of Who It is and He said, "My son, what are you searching for?" I sat up and said, "Money!" He said, "Did you not hear Me when I spoke to you? Do you think My Word is a joke to you? I told you in Ecclesiastes that whoever loves money never has money enough. And whoever loves wealth, is never satisfied with his income. But I also told you to seek Me first. I told you to delight yourself in Me. Are you doing that? Or are you moving back towards the world?" As if coming out of a trance, tears flowing, I regained focus and looked up to where my hope is and I said, "thank You!"

I got dressed for the day and jumped in the Equinox with eager thoughts of who's coming to visit me tonight. Despite knowing I need to be seeking my life mate, my thoughts were more into thinking who I'd like to date and plus, I like the chase! Befriending beautiful women is something special! I mean, I want to go through that threshold… one day. But if I keep getting texts telling me to come play, that's going to delay the process! Suddenly I hear that voice again saying, "Stop this!" I swerved to avoid hitting a curve, and sternly and more firmly the voice said to me, "My son, what are you searching for?" I pulled over to gather my senses and direct my attention to this dialogue. I said, "I want a woman who loves You first, who's my best friend, who's beautiful on the outside and within. One who's meant for me and me for her where no cheating occurs on either side" and He replied, "You're not ready. You're motivated by fornication and I commanded you not to! I told you the marriage bed should be kept pure, but you defile it with stains of sin and with a shameless grin you are proud of your immorality. Do not be conformed to evil desires my son, for you are no longer ignorant and this is it. For, even though I love you, I will judge you!" I drove off with watery pupils again, knowing I need to repent but shame had been my excuse and self blame had been my refusal, so I hadn't yet. Cruising through the city of Memphis, I'm convinced this intensive display of guidance from on high was meant for my direction and correction, but I know I've been doing wrong. And I want to get on His path, and I want to stay committed but I'm embarrassed and I admit it. And forgiveness is what I long for, but I can't even forgive myself!

So I needed some alone time to unload my mind and get back to a place of peace. I pulled up at a park and released what's been ailing me, the anger, the anxiety, and the sadness, all that resides in me from frustration to emptiness. And in my tantrum and complaining The Lord had been restraining His anger but He had heard enough and He said, "My son, what are you searching for? How could you be in need when I am your provider? How would you even breathe if I had no desire to care for you? I am your refuge! I am your strength! I am your friend, but you want to befriend the world! You're squandering your inheritance! All I want you to do is stay with me, but you won't even pray to me unless you need my assistance! And even in that, I insisted because you are My son! If you want My favor, then start back praying! If you want forgiveness, it starts with repentance! If you're seeking answers then start fasting! If you want my spirit, then start asking! I sacrificed My Son for you! That's how you should know my love for you! And I'm not done with you because you're still under My grace and My mercy! But what hurts me is that you don't believe. Am I not all that you need?" And that was my confirmation, my moment of clarity, my revelation. I smiled at the Heavens and reciprocated the question I was asked before, but now it's rhetorical as I responded, "You're right, what am I searching for?"